A SONG FOR JOSEPH

A Christmas Story for Children

Written by: Mervin A. Marquardt
Illustrated by: Bill Heuer

ARCH Books

Copyright © 1981 CONCORDIA PUBLISHING HOUSE
ST. LOUIS, MISSOURI
MANUFACTURED IN THE UNITED STATES OF AMERICA
ALL RIGHTS RESERVED
ISBN 0-570-06146-6

Sing me a song of a man named Joseph;
Sing me a song of that carpenter-man:
Husband of Mary, God's honorary
Father of Jesus—a heavenly plan!

Saw on your wood, O Joseph, Joseph;
Saw on your wood with all of your might.
Crib for a baby, rocking chair maybe,
Plane it and paint it for sale tonight.

Why aren't you married to anyone, Joseph?
Why aren't you married to anyone here?
"I've got a girl, best in the world;
I'm going to marry Mary my dear.

"Mary will have a dear little baby;
Mary will have the sign of God's love!
Mary's dear child, gentle and mild,
Will come to the world from heaven above.

"Mary saw an angel sent from heaven;
Mary saw an angel and so did I.
His message was clear: 'Don't you fear;
The Baby is the Son of God on high!'"

Where are you going, O Joseph, Joseph?
Where are you going this beautiful day
With corn and candles, blankets and sandals?
Mary and Joseph, oh, can't you stay?

"We're going to Bethlehem down in Judah;
We're going to Bethlehem, David's town.
Sisters and brothers, fathers and mothers—
All of the family is traveling down."

Why are you going, O Joseph, Joseph?
Why are you going so far away?
Animals wild could threaten the child;
The trip is too dangerous! Please delay!

"Caesar demanded that we be counted;
Caesar demanded that all the earth—
High or low—we should go
Back to the town of our family's birth."

How are you going, O Joseph, Joseph?
How are you going to carry that load?
"A donkey will hold us; God will enfold us
Traveling down the Jerusalem Road."

Where will you stay, O Joseph, Joseph?
Where will you stay in Bethlehem town?
I know for a fact that the inn is so packed
There's hardly a bed for a king with a crown!

"God will provide us; He is beside us;
God will provide us and give us His best—
If only a stable, no bed or a table—
God will provide us a haven of rest."

Mary and Joseph and all their possessions,
Mary and Joseph begin on their way,
Jerusalem slighting, at Bethlehem lighting,
Asking the innkeeper where they can stay.

Joseph is saying that Mary is pregnant;
Joseph is saying the baby is due.
"No room in the inn," says the man with a grin,
"But there is a place where you'll make do."

Joseph and Mary are led to a stable—
Joseph and Mary with cattle and sheep!
Clean it and preen it and give it a sheen;
Hurry, O Joseph, while Mary's asleep!

We sing a song of a man named Joseph;
We sing a song of that carpenter-man:
Husband of Mary, God's honorary
Father of Jesus—a heavenly plan!

Joseph, help Mary! The miracle's coming!
Joseph, help Mary give birth to her son!
Shout with a cheer! Jesus is here!
Tickle His ear! His life is begun!

Saw on your wood, O Joseph, Joseph;
Saw on your wood with all of your might.
Crib for the Baby, rocking chair maybe,
Plane it and paint it for Baby tonight.

Who are those people, O Joseph, Joseph?
Who are those people approaching your door?
Magi at mangers? Those shepherds are strangers!
I'm certain that no one has seen them before!

"These are the ones who are specially chosen;
These are the ones who know Jesus as Lord.
A star in the sky and the angels on high
Brought them all here our Lord to adore."

"How about you, O Singer, Singer?
How about you? Won't you sing too?
Praises to Jesus who came to please us!
Praises to Jesus who pleases you!"

Sing me a song of a man named Joseph;
Sing me a song of a carpenter-man.
Husband of Mary, God's honorary
Father of Jesus—a heavenly plan!

DEAR PARENT:

Although the Christmas story may be familiar to your child, the story is usually told from the perspective of Jesus' mother, the shepherds, or the Wise Men (the Magi). Joseph, however, has our attention in this presentation of (primarily) Luke 2:1-7.

In order to make this telling somewhat more complete, the account alludes to the angel's visit to Mary (Luke 1:26-38), the angel's visit to Joseph (Matthew 1:18-25), the arrival of the shepherds (Luke 2:8-16), and the arrival of the Magi (Matthew 2:10-11).

After reading this version of the Christmas story, help your child take up the invitation to be a singer who praises God for the gift of His Son. Ask your child which Christmas hymns he or she would like to sing; suggest some easy ones of your own. Your child might even enjoy singing his or her own melody to the words in the book.

As your child understands who Joseph was, ask how Joseph might have felt at different points in the story:

thinking about his work and forthcoming marriage;

hearing the message of the angel;

getting ready to leave his home and take his new wife on a dangerous trip;

almost being a failure at providing a place to stay in Bethlehem; and

rejoicing over the birth of Jesus.

Help your child to feel the joy felt by Joseph and Mary—and the shepherds and Magi—when they realized that God loved them and had sent them the Savior of the world. Help your child feel that same joy, for the Savior born in Bethlehem is your child's Savior too.

THE EDITOR